AMAZING MAMMALS

By Honor Head

Gareth Stevens
Publishing

Please visit our web site at www.garethstevens.com.
For a free catalog describing our list of high-quality books, call 1-800-542-2595 (USA)
or 1-800-387-3178 (Canada). Our fax: 1-877-542-2596

Library of Congress Cataloging-in-Publication Data
Head, Honor.
    Amazing mammals / Honor Head.
        p. cm. — (Amazing life cycles)
    Includes index.
    ISBN-13: 978-0-8368-8896-6 (lib. bdg.)
    ISBN-10: 0-8368-8896-0 (lib. bdg.)
     1. Mammals—Juvenile literature.   2. Mammals—Life cycles—Juvenile
literature. I. Title.
    QL706.2.H43   2008
    599—dc22   2007043754

This North American edition first published in 2008 by
Gareth Stevens Publishing
A Weekly Reader® Company
1 Reader's Digest Road
Pleasantville, NY 10570-7000 USA

This U.S. edition copyright © 2008 by Gareth Stevens, Inc. Original edition copyright © 2007 by ticktock Media Ltd.
First published in Great Britain in 2007 by ticktock Media Ltd., Unit 2, Orchard Business Centre, North Farm Road,
Tunbridge Wells, Kent, TN2 3XF United Kingdom

ticktock Project Editor: Ruth Owen
ticktock Project Designer: Sara Greasley
With thanks to: Sally Morgan, Jean Coppendale, and Elizabeth Wiggans

Gareth Stevens Senior Editor: Brian Fitzgerald
Gareth Stevens Creative Director: Lisa Donovan
Gareth Stevens Graphic Designer: Alex Davis

Photo credits (t = top; b = bottom; c = center; l = left; r = right):
Ardea: 28c. Corbis: 20 main, 21t, 31t. FLPA: 5t, 7b, 9tr, 9tl, 13 main, 15cl, 16tl, 16c, 21b, 25c, 26 main. Jupiter Images: 18tl.
Nature Picture Library: 16–17 main. NHPA: 30b. Oxford Scientific Photo Library: 10 main, 17t, 18c. Shutterstock: cover, title
page, contents page, 4tl, 4tr, 5b, 6t, 7t, 8tl, 10tl, 11t, 11b, 12tl, 12 main, 13t, 14tl, 14tr, 14cl, 14b, 14–15c, 15tl, 15tr, 15cr, 15b, 20tl,
22tl, 23t, 23 main, 24tl, 24–25 main, 25t, 26tl, 27t, 27b, 28tl, 29b, 30tl, 31 main. Superstock: 4l, 9 main, 18–19 main, 22b,
30c. Terry Hardie – www.orcaresearch.org: 8 main. ticktock image archive: map page 6. Wendy Blanshard, Australian
Koala Foundation, www.savethekoala.com: 29t.

Printed in the United States of America

1 2 3 4 5 6 7 8 9 10 09 08 07

Contents

Words in the glossary appear in **bold type** the first time they are used in the text.

What Is a Mammal?

This hairy cow is a mammal.

A mammal is a **vertebrate**. Vertebrates are animals that have a backbone. Mammals are **warm-blooded**. Their body temperature stays about the same no matter how hot or cold the air or water is around them.

Most mammals give birth to live babies. When a mammal baby is born, the mother feeds it with milk from inside her body.

A hairy hippo nose!

Mammals also have hair on their bodies. A hippopotamus is a mammal with smooth skin, but it has hair in its ears and on its nose.

A mother leopard feeds her cubs.

A tiny pipistrelle bat sits on a scientist's finger.

Most mammals live on land, but some live in water. All mammals use lungs to breathe.

Mammals can be tiny, like a pipistrelle bat, or huge, like an elephant!

Did you know that people are mammals, too?

Mammal Habitats

A **habitat** is the place where a plant or an animal lives. Mammals live in hot desert habitats and cold, icy habitats, such as the Arctic. The ocean is a habitat. Mammals such as whales and seals live there.

Polar bears are mammals that live in the icy, snowy Arctic.

Mammals can be found in every habitat around the world.

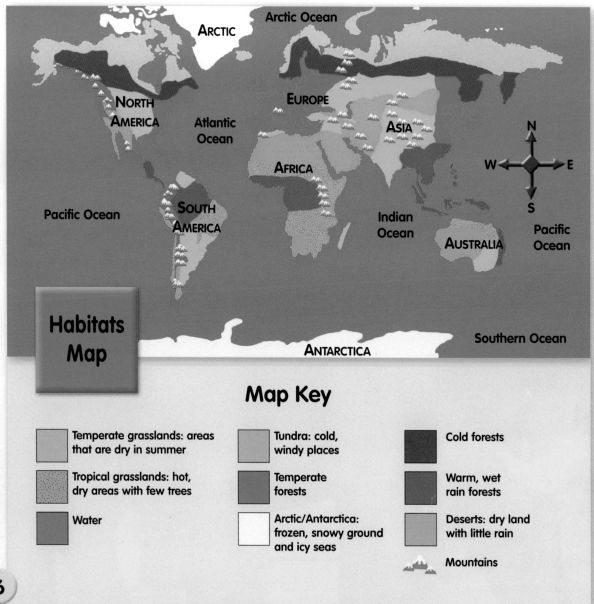

Habitats Map

Arctic Ocean

ARCTIC

NORTH AMERICA

Atlantic Ocean

EUROPE

ASIA

AFRICA

SOUTH AMERICA

Indian Ocean

AUSTRALIA

Pacific Ocean

Pacific Ocean

ANTARCTICA

Southern Ocean

N
W E
S

Map Key

Temperate grasslands: areas that are dry in summer	
Tropical grasslands: hot, dry areas with few trees	
Water	
Tundra: cold, windy places	
Temperate forests	
Arctic/Antarctica: frozen, snowy ground and icy seas	
Cold forests	
Warm, wet rain forests	
Deserts: dry land with little rain	
Mountains	

Rain forests are warm, wet habitats with many trees and plants. Mammals such as monkeys, gorillas, and sloths live there.

Grasslands are hot, dry habitats. Mammals such as rhinos, elephants, giraffes, and meerkats live on the grasslands in Africa.

Sloths hang upside down from branches. The baby rides on its mother's chest.

AMAZING MAMMAL FACT
The rhinoceros gets its name from its horn. In Greek, *rhino* means "nose" and *ceros* means "horn."

A rhinoceros calf feeds on milk from its mother.

Meat-Eating Mammals

Animals that eat meat are called **carnivores**. Most carnivores have sharp claws and teeth to help them catch and eat their **prey**. Animals that hunt prey are called **predators**.

Big cats such as tigers and cheetahs are carnivores.

AMAZING MAMMAL FACT
Orcas are also called killer whales because they feed on seals, penguins, and even other whales!

Orcas sometimes surf onto a beach to catch seals and other prey. The waves then pull the whales back out to sea.

The giant anteater uses its long, sharp claws to tear a hole in a **termite** nest or an ant nest. The anteater then puts its long, sticky tongue in the hole and scoops up its prey.

A termite nest

Bats are **nocturnal**. They sleep during the day and hunt at night. Skunks and foxes are other nocturnal mammals.

A pipistrelle bat hunts a moth.

Meerkats have sharp claws so they can dig for worms and other small prey.

Meerkats chase and catch scorpions and lizards.

Before a meerkat eats a **scorpion**, it bites off the scorpion's stinger.

Plant-Eating Mammals

Every koala lives in its own home tree.

Animals that eat only plants are called **herbivores**. They eat leaves, roots, fruit, or flowers. Some herbivores have developed special ways to help them eat the food they need.

Hippos live in Africa. During the day, they keep cool in rivers. They come out of the river at sunset to eat grass during the night.

AMAZING MAMMAL FACT
Hippos use their wide lips to grab grass. Then they swing their heads from side to side to pull up the grass by the roots.

Koalas eat only one type of food—the leaves of the eucalyptus (yoo-kuh-LIP-tuhss) tree. These trees grow in Australia, where koalas live.

Koalas spend their time eating and sleeping in eucalyptus trees.

Warthogs use their strong snouts to dig up the hard ground and find tasty underground roots.

Warthogs live on African grasslands.

Koala dads don't help care for their babies.

Mom Meets Dad

Some male and female mammals **mate** and then bring up their young together. After other types of mammals mate, however, the female cares for the babies alone or with other females in a group.

In meerkat family groups, only one male and one female become a couple. They are the only members of the group allowed to mate.

AMAZING MAMMAL FACT
Meerkats live in big family groups of about 30 animals.

After a male and female warthog have mated, the male leaves. Adult male warthogs live on their own.

Male warthogs fight over who gets to mate with a female.

AMAZING MAMMAL FACT
Orcas stay with their mothers all their lives. They live in family groups called pods.

When a male orca is fully grown and ready to mate, he goes to another pod and mates with a female. Then he goes back to live with his mother in his family group. The female orca raises her babies in her own family group.

Orca couples swim around each other, as if they were dancing!

A baby lion is called a cub.

What Is a Life Cycle?

A **life cycle** is the different stages that an animal or a plant goes through in its life. This diagram shows the usual life cycle of a mammal.

1

Female mammals give birth to live babies.

THE LIFE CYCLE OF A LION

6

When they become adults, male and female mammals meet and mate.

5

Some mammals live with their family group when they grow up. Others go off and live on their own.

Amazing Mammal Life Cycles

Orca

In the pages that follow, we will learn about the life cycles of some amazing mammals—from orcas in the sea to koalas in the treetops.

Koala

2

Female mammals feed their babies milk.

3

Lions are carnivores. A lion family group is called a pride.

The mothers care for their babies. Sometimes the fathers help, too.

4

Mammals teach their babies how to find food. Young carnivores practice their hunting skills on each other.

Pipistrelle Bat

Pipistrelle bats usually have one baby each year. Hundreds of female bats gather to give birth in a place with a lot of space, such as a barn. Sometimes they gather under a bridge or in a cave.

Father bats do not help look after the babies.

A baby bat is called a pup. When the pups are born, they stay together with their mothers in a huge group called a nursery roost.

Bat pup

Mother bat

LIFE CYCLE FACTS

Female pipistrelle bats start to have babies when they are between 6 and 12 months old. They are pregnant for about 50 days.

Bat pup

A newborn pup clings to its mother's fur as she carries the pup from one place to another place.

A mother bat can find her own pup among hundreds of other bats. She knows its smell and its sound.

A mother bat feeds its pup.

Pups can fly by themselves when they are about two to four weeks old. They leave their mothers when they are eight weeks old.

Pipistrelle bats pack together tightly in a nursery roost.

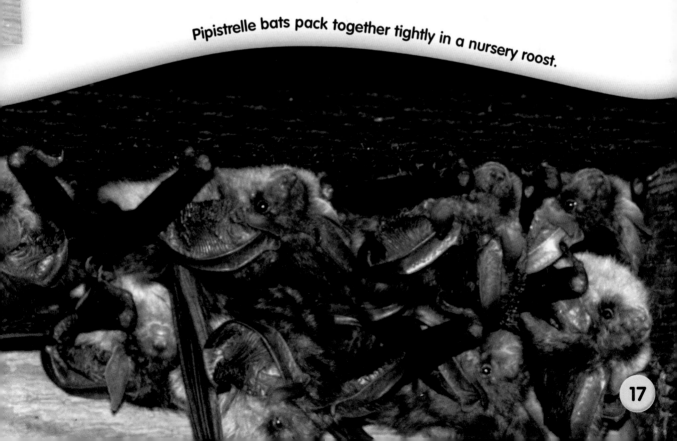

Giant Anteater

Giant anteaters live on dry grasslands in South America. Adult giant anteaters live alone. After the male and female mate, the male leaves, and the female cares for the baby.

An anteater's claws can be 4 inches (10 centimeters) long.

An anteater can use its tail like another leg for support.

The female giant anteater gives birth standing up on her back legs.

The baby anteater is born with fur and sharp claws. The baby crawls onto its mother's back, where she licks it clean.

After a few months, the baby hops off its mother's back to explore and then hops on again.

LIFE CYCLE FACTS
Female giant anteaters start to have babies when they are about three years old. Females are pregnant for about 190 days.

The baby stays with its mother until it is about two years old.

If the baby falls off, it grunts to let its mother know.

19

Orca

Baby orcas, called calves, are born underwater. They are born tail first. An orca calf can be nearly 8 feet (2.4 meters) long when it is born!

A newborn orca weighs 400 pounds (180 kilograms).

As soon as a calf is born, its mother pushes the baby to the surface to take its first breath of air.

LIFE CYCLE FACTS

Female orcas start to have babies when they are about 15 years old. Females are pregnant for 15 to 18 months.

The mother orca uses her flippers and nose to guide her calf to the surface of the water.

Calf

Flipper

An orca calf feeds on its mother's milk for the first one to two years of its life.

The mother orca teaches the calf how to hunt and catch food.

Most orca pods have about 30 members.

Orca families "talk" to each other using grunts, whistles, and squeals. Calves learn how to make these noises.

The meerkat's dark eye rings protect its eyes from bright sunlight.

Meerkat

Meerkats live in large family groups with their kits, or babies. Meerkats live in underground homes called **burrows**.

LIFE CYCLE FACTS

Female meerkats start to have babies when they are one year old. Females are pregnant for about 75 days.

Female meerkats have three to five kits at a time. Kits stay in the burrow until they are three to four weeks old.

Adult meerkats take turns babysitting while the others go out to hunt.

Meerkats stand up on their back legs to watch for predators.

When kits are about one month old, they start to go on hunting trips. Each kit has its own adult that teaches it how to hunt.

23

Warthog

The female warthog gives birth to two or three babies at one time in an underground burrow. The babies, or piglets, leave the burrow when they are about two weeks old.

Warthogs use their good sense of smell to find food.

Newborn piglets need to stay warm and dry. To stay dry, they sleep on a raised shelf at the back of the burrow.

LIFE CYCLE FACTS
Female warthogs start to have babies when they are 18 months old. Females are pregnant for six months.

Adult warthogs and older piglets enjoy a mud bath to cool off on a hot day.

Both male and female warthogs have **tusks**. Warthogs use their sharp tusks to fight off lions and other predators.

Warthog piglets are not born with tusks. The tusks grow as the babies gets older.

Mothers feed their piglets for about four months. Male piglets stay with their mother for about two years. Females go off on their own when they are about 18 months old.

Hippopotamus

Hippos live in groups called herds. A herd includes one adult male, many females, and their young. When a female is ready to give birth, she looks for a soft spot at the edge of the river.

Male hippos fight over females.

The hippo baby, or calf, is born in shallow water at the edge of the river. The mother quickly pushes the baby to the surface so it can breathe.

LIFE CYCLE FACTS
Female hippos start to have babies when they are nine years old. Females are pregnant for eight months.

The mother and calf stay away from the herd for the first couple of weeks. This stops one of the other adults from accidentally hurting the baby.

An adult female hippo weighs 1.5 tons. That's more than many cars weigh!

When most hippos grow up, they stay in the herd in which they were born. A male hippo may start his own herd when he is about 20 years old.

AMAZING MAMMAL FACT
Sometimes a hippo calf will rest on its mother's back. It will slip into the water if it gets too hot and then climb back on.

Koala

Koalas are **marsupials** (mahr-SOO-pee-uhlz). The mother has a pouch on her tummy where her baby lives. The pouch is like a big pocket. A newborn koala is called a joey.

The female koala gives birth in a eucalyptus tree.

LIFE CYCLE FACTS

Female koalas start to have babies when they are two years old. Females are pregnant for 35 days.

A newborn joey is about the size of a jellybean.

The newborn joey is tiny! It has no hair, ears, or eyes. It crawls into its mother's pouch. In the pouch, the joey drinks its mother's milk.

The joey gets bigger and bigger. Over the next few months, its fur, ears, and eyes grow. When the joey is six to seven months old, it starts to ride on its mother's back.

Joey

When the koala is about one year old, it leaves its mother. This is usually when the mother gives birth to another joey.

That's Amazing!

All mammal mothers care for their babies. They feed them milk and teach them how to find food. But mammal babies begin life in a lot of different ways!

A baby giraffe is called a calf.

Female polar bears **hibernate** in a den for the winter. While they are in the den, they give birth to their babies, called cubs.

The polar bear's den is under the snow. The bear's white coat helps it blend in with the snow.

AMAZING MAMMAL FACT
Newborn polar bear cubs are about 12 inches (30 cm) long. They are blind, pink, and hairless.

The mother and cubs leave the den in spring, four to five months after the cubs are born.

The female platypus lays two or three grape-size eggs. The eggs **hatch** about 12 days later. The baby platypuses drink milk from their mother.

The giraffe is the world's tallest animal. The female gives birth standing up. Its calf drops more than 6 feet (2 m) to the ground!

A newborn giraffe is taller than most humans!

Glossary

burrows: underground tunnels and holes where some animals live

carnivores: animals or plants that eat meat

habitat: the natural conditions in which a plant or an animal lives

hatch: to break out of an egg

herbivores: animals that do not eat meat

hibernate: a long sleep during which an animal's body temperature drops and its heart rate slows

life cycle: the series of changes that an animal or a plant goes through in its life

marsupials: animals that carry their young in pouches on their bodies

mate: to come together to make eggs or babies

nocturnal: active at night

predators: animals that hunt and kill other animals for food

prey: animals that are hunted by other animals as food

scorpion: a small animal with eight legs, two arms with big claws, and a tail with a poisonous sting

termite: an insect that is like a large ant. Termites live in big groups.

tusks: long, sharp pointed teeth

vertebrate: an animal that has a backbone

warm-blooded: describes an animal whose body temperature stays the same no matter how hot or cold the air or water is around it

Index